150 Full-Color Art Nouveau Patterns and Designs

Friedrich Wolfrum and Co.

DOVER PUBLICATIONS, INC.
Mineola, New York

Note

Artists, illustrators and craftspeople will appreciate the quality, diversity, and imaginative flair of these rare Art Nouveau patterns and designs. Selected from a vintage turn-of-the century portfolio, the designs feature swirling, sensuous floral and foliate motifs that are a hallmark of the Art Nouveau style. They are reproduced here in vibrant full color, providing a rich source of artistic and creative inspiration for anyone working in the decorative arts, interior design, and a host of other arts and crafts endeavors.

Bibliographical Note

This Dover edition, first published in 2005, is an original selection of plates from a portfolio published by Friedrich Wolfrum and Co., Vienna, n.d.

Library of Congress Cataloging-in-Publication Data

150 full-color art nouveau patterns and designs / Friedrich Wolfrum and Co.
    p. cm. — (Dover pictorial archive series)
  An original selection of plates from a portfolio originally published by Friedrich Wolfrum and Co., Vienna.
    ISBN 0-486-44511-9 (pbk.)
    1. Decoration and ornament—Austria—Vienna—Art nouveau. I. Title: One hundred fifty full-color art nouveau patterns and designs. II. Friedrich Wolfrum and Co. (Vienna, Austria) III. Series.

NK1380.A115 2005
745.4'09436'1309034—dc22

2005049242

Manufactured in the United States of America
Dover Publications, Inc., 31 East 2nd Street, Mineola, N.Y. 11501

I

2

5

8

9

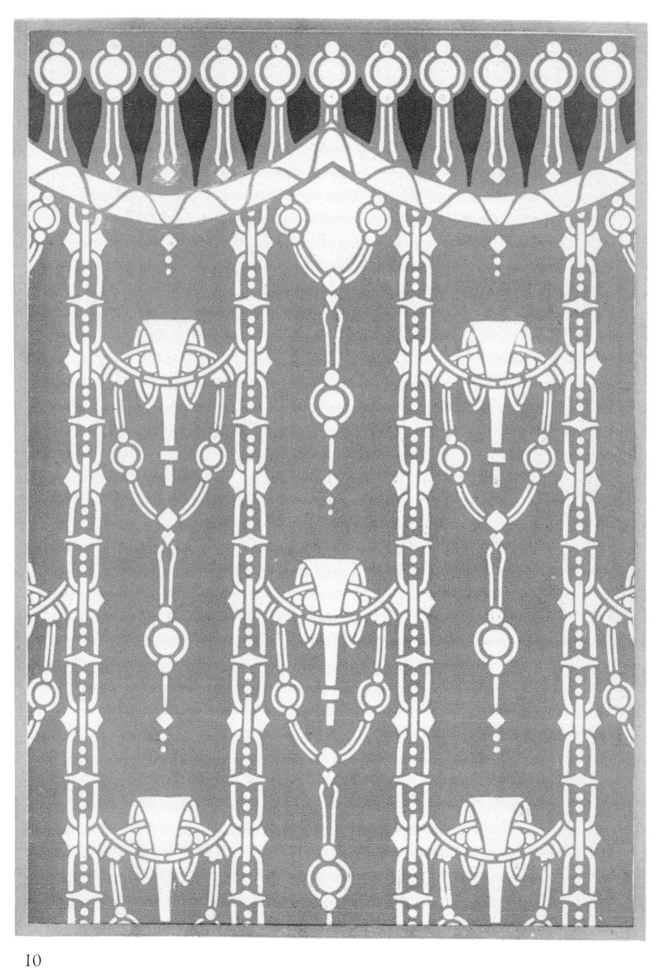

10

11

12

13

14

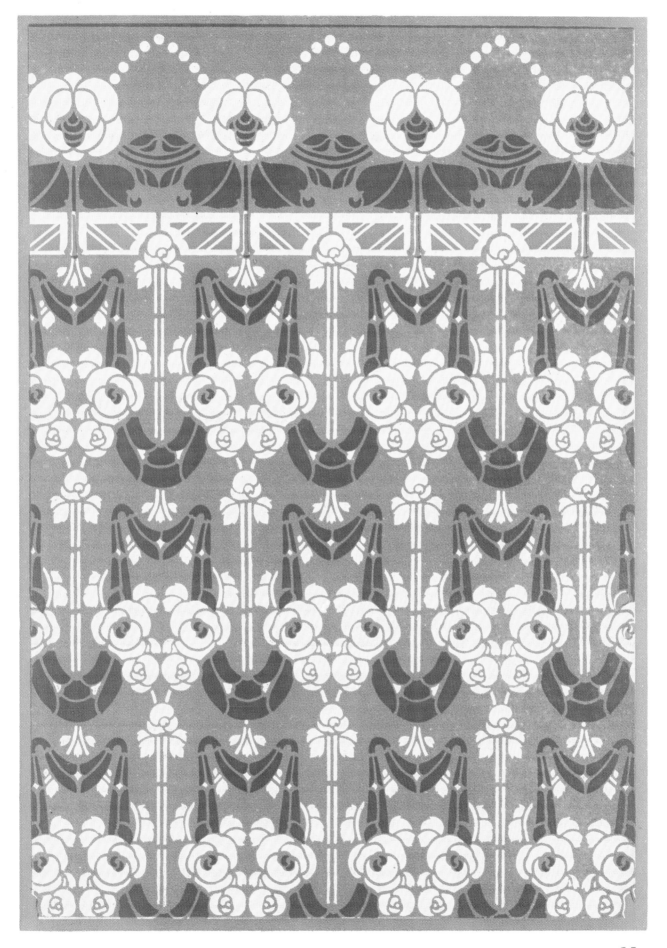

15

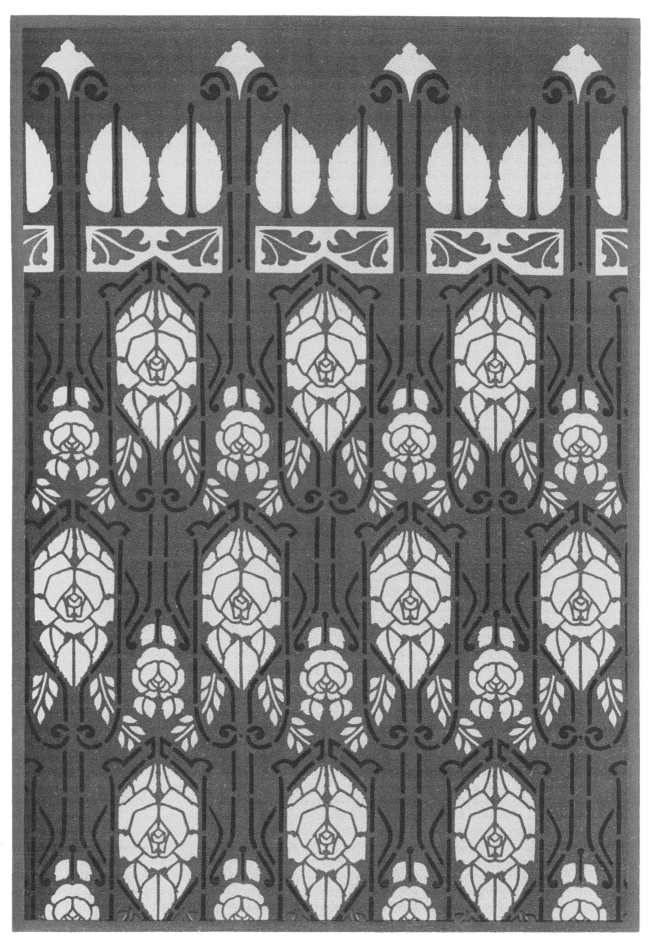

16

18

19

20

21

22

24

26

27

28

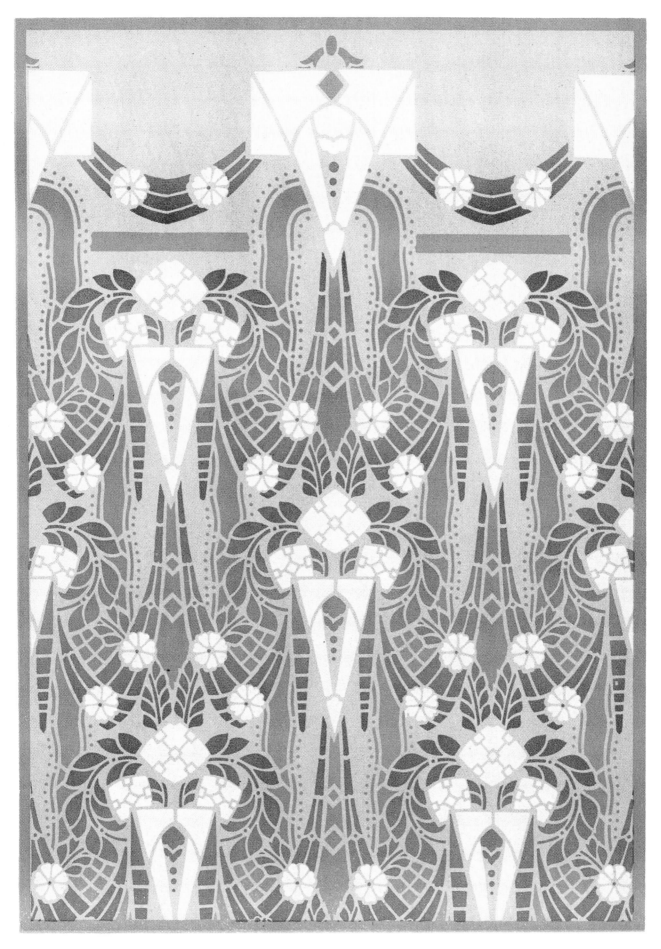

29

31

32

33

36

37

38

40

41

43

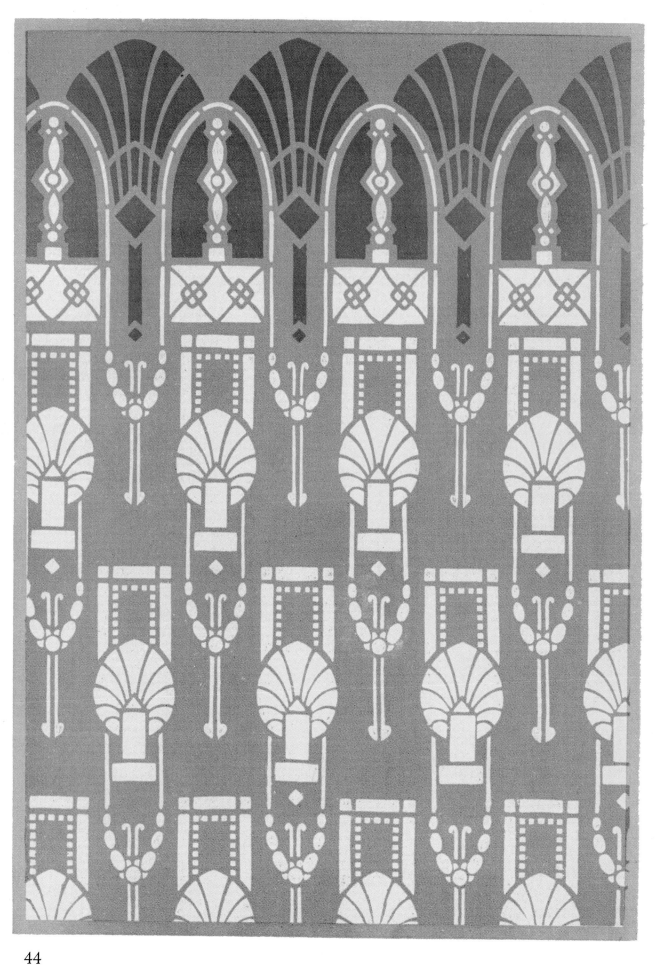

44

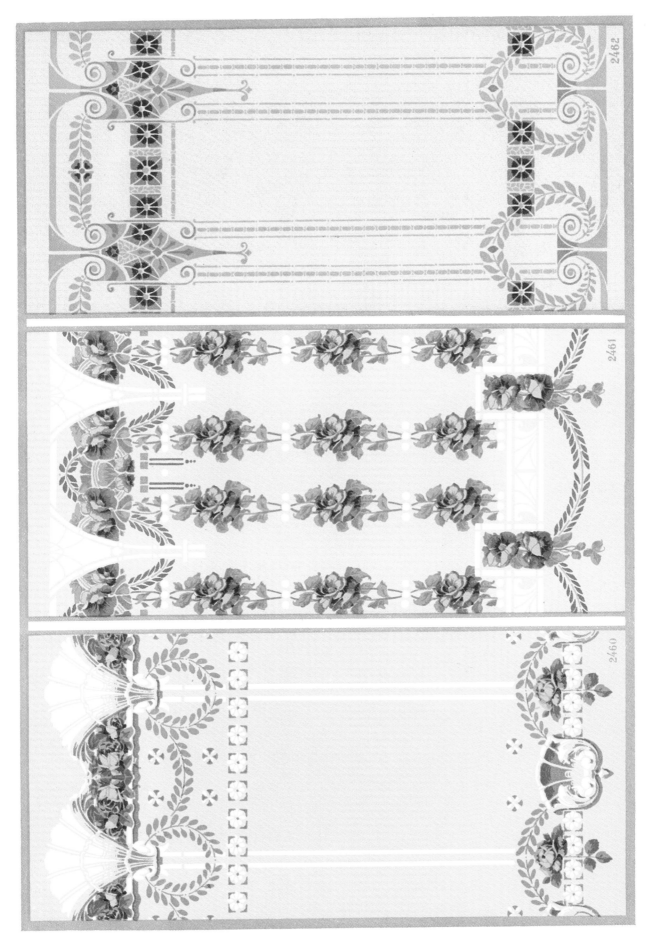

48

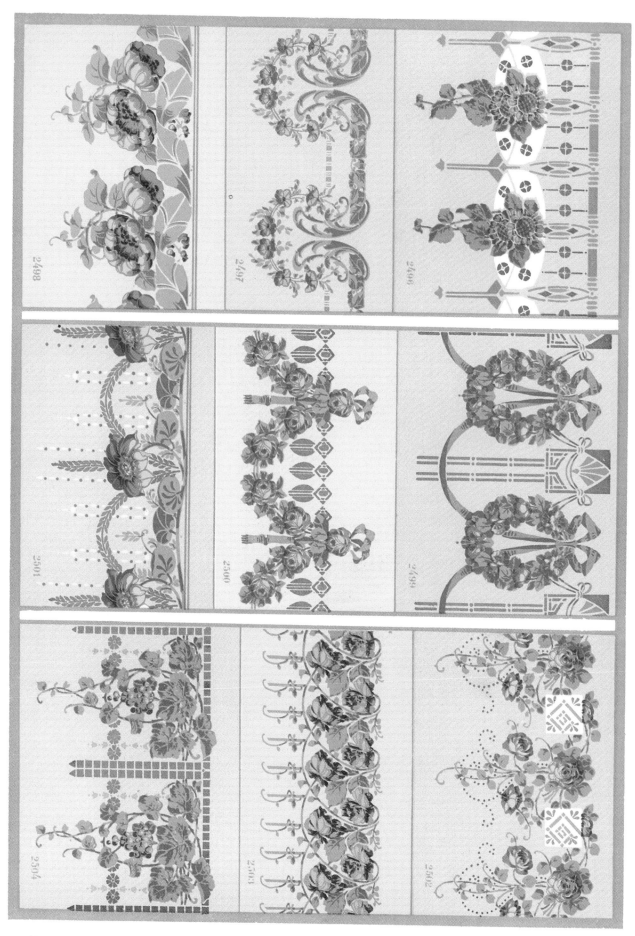

50

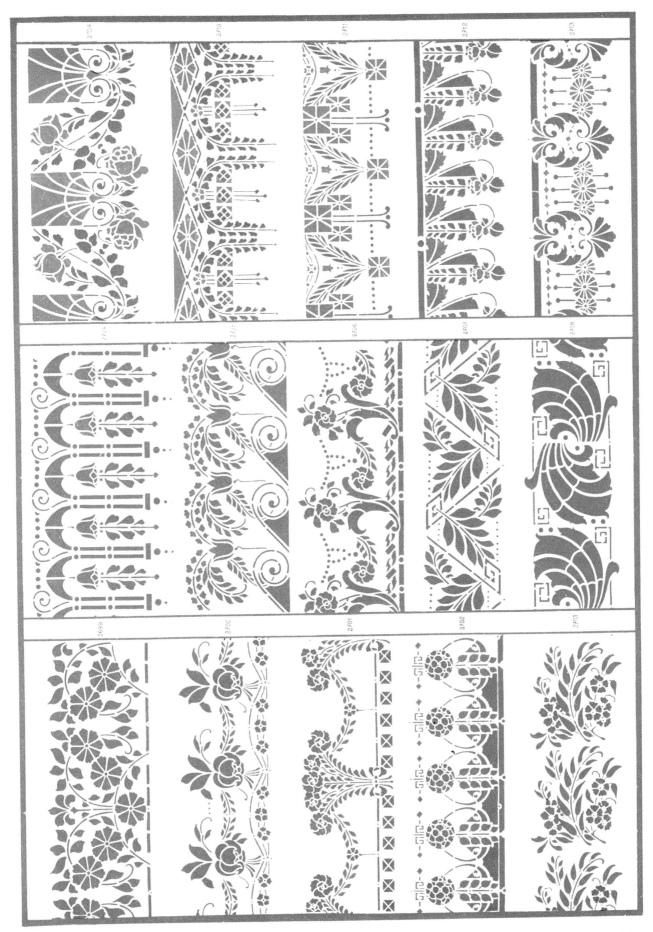

51

52

53

54

55

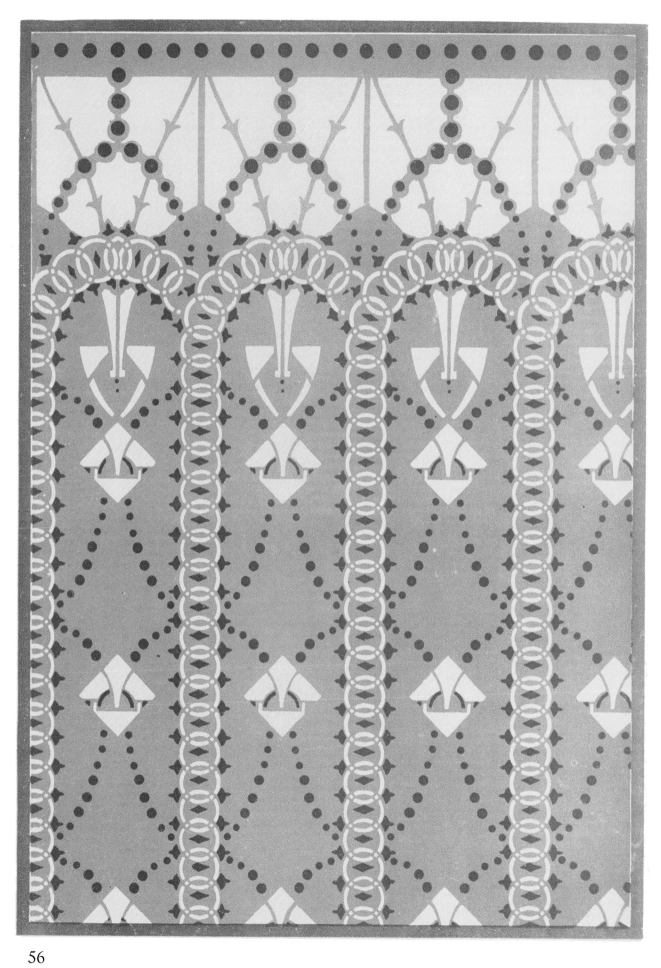

56

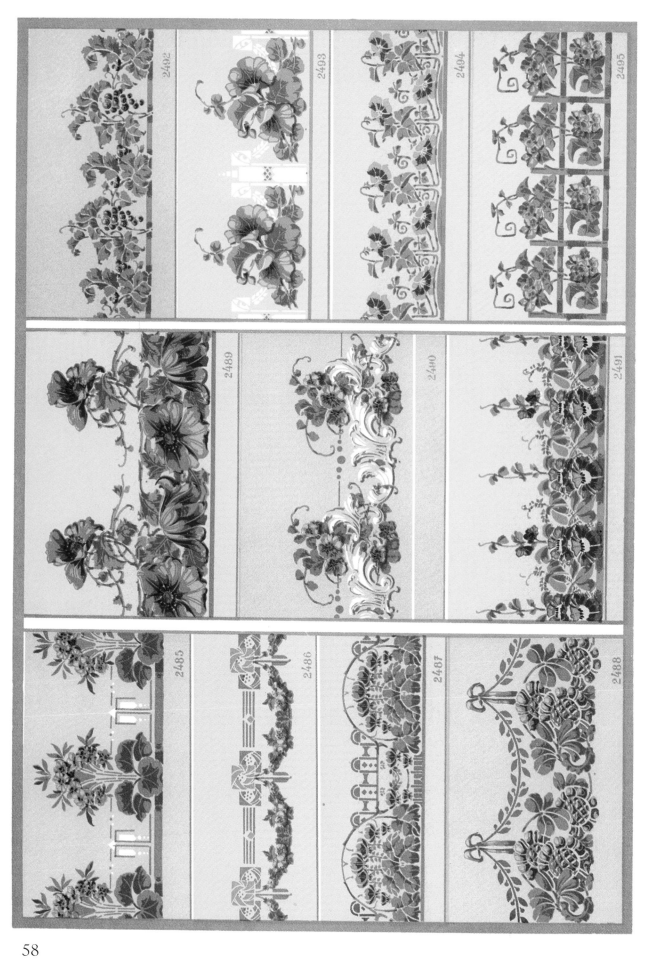

2492

2493

2494

2495

2489

2490

2491

2485

2486

2487

2488

58

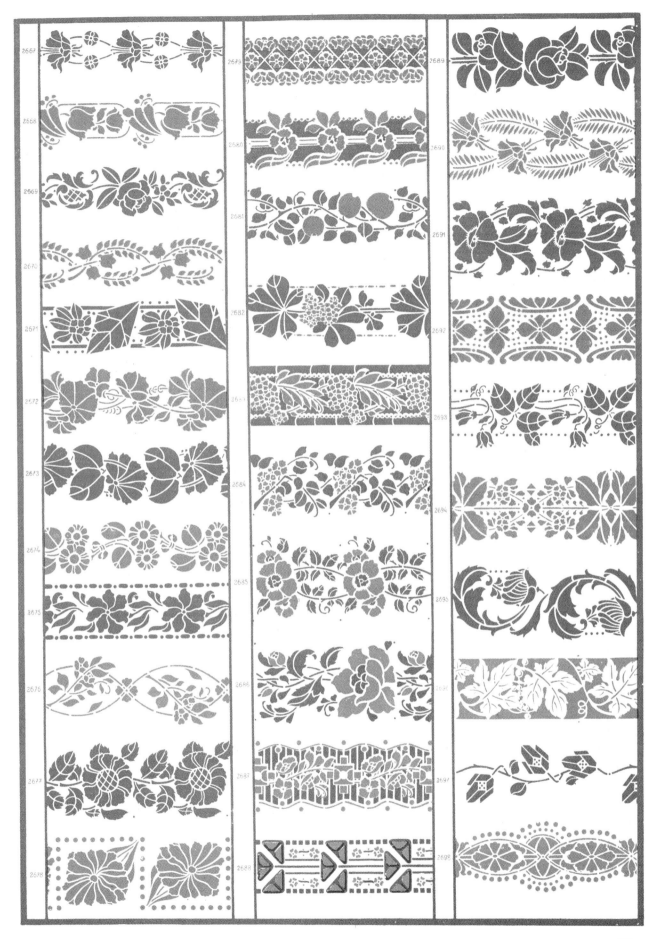